P9-DMZ-538

FEARLESS

IMAGINE YOUR LIFE WITHOUT FEAR

SMALL GROUP
DISCUSSION GUIDE

FEARLESS

IMAGINE YOUR LIFE WITHOUT FEAR

SMALL GROUP
DISCUSSION GUIDE

Max Lucado

THOMAS NELSON
Since 1798

NASHVILLE   DALLAS   MEXICO CITY   RIO DE JANEIRO   BEIJING

© 2009 by Max Lucado

All rights reserved. No portion of this book may be reproduced, stored in a retrieval system, or transmitted in any form or by any means—electronic, mechanical, photocopy, recording, scanning, or other—except for brief quotations in critical reviews or articles, without the prior written permission of the publisher.

Published in Nashville, Tennessee, by Thomas Nelson. Thomas Nelson is a registered trademark of Thomas Nelson, Inc.

The publisher is grateful to Kate Etue for her writing skills and collaboration in developing the content for this book.

Thomas Nelson, Inc., titles may be purchased in bulk for educational, business, fund-raising, or sales promotional use. For information, please e-mail SpecialMarkets@ thomasnelson.com.

All Scripture quotations, unless otherwise indicated, are taken from THE NEW KING JAMES VERSION. Copyright © 1982 by Thomas Nelson, Inc. Used by permission. All rights reserved.

Scripture quotations marked NASB are taken from NEW AMERICAN STANDARD BIBLE®, © Copyright The Lockman Foundation 1960, 1962, 1963, 1968, 1971, 1972, 1973, 1975, 1977, 1995. Used by permission.

Scripture quotations marked NCV are taken from New Century Version®. Copyright © 2005 by Thomas Nelson, Inc. Used by permission. All rights reserved.

Scripture quotations marked NLT are taken from the Holy Bible, New Living Translation, copyright © 1996, 2004. Used by permission of Tyndale House Publishers, Inc., Wheaton, Illinois 60189. All rights reserved.

Scripture quotations marked NIV are taken from the HOLY BIBLE: NEW INTERNATIONAL VERSION®. Copyright © 1973, 1978, 1984 by International Bible Society. Used by permission of Zondervan Publishing House. All rights reserved.

Scripture quotations marked RSV are taken from the REVISED STANDARD VERSION of the Bible. Copyright © 1946, 1952, 1971, 1973 by the Division of Christian Education of the National Council of the Churches of Christ in the U.S.A. Used by permission.

ISBN: 978-1-4185-4271-9

Printed in the United States of America
09 10 11 12 13 RRD 6 5 4 3 2

CONTENTS

WHY ARE YOU FEARFUL, O YOU OF LITTLE FAITH?

Matthew 8:26

INTRODUCTION

They're talking layoffs at work, slowdowns in the economy, flare-ups in the Middle East, turnovers at headquarters, downturns in the housing market, upswings in global warming. The plague of our day, terrorism, begins with the word *terror*. Fear, it seems, has taken up a hundred-year lease on the building next door and set up shop. Oversized and rude, fear herds us into a prison of unlocked doors. Wouldn't it be great to walk out?

Imagine your life, wholly untouched by angst. What if faith, not fear, was your default reaction to threats? If you could hover a fear magnet over your heart and extract every last shaving of dread, insecurity, or doubt, what would remain? Envision a day, just one day, where you could trust more and fear less.

Can you imagine your life without fear?

HOW THIS STUDY WORKS

Each week you will be asked to do some preparatory work at home before you meet together as a group. By reading the chapter from *Fearless* that corresponds with the week's study, you will gain a better understanding of the material and will be able to contribute more to your group discussion (see the Reading Schedule for *Fearless* on page 13). Please commit to doing your "homework" before you meet—you and your group will benefit the most when everyone agrees to participate fully.

Each week's study is broken into five sections. They are all key parts of growing closer to God and loosening your grip on fear. The READ sections of each chapter explain what to read at home, and they give a brief summary of the main points in those chapters. The REFLECT sections are intended to get you into the Word so you can study the topic before the discussion starts. That way everyone will have had time to think deeply about these concepts before talking them over with the group. And the DISCUSS sections are just that— questions for you to discuss and explore together as a group. You don't have to answer those at home beforehand unless you want to. Finally, we'll leave you with some ideas for continuing the application of these truths in the WRAP UP section at the end of each chapter. And each week ends with a MEMORY

VERSE. As you write God's words on your heart, you will grow in your knowledge and understanding of him.

Finally, approach your group discussion time with a mind-set of openness and vulnerability. While the focus of this study is on fear and living in the abundant freedom Jesus promises his followers, an equal purpose for your group is to grow in community and intimacy with one another. If you hold back in the discussions, refusing to let your real self be known, your group will suffer. God made you the way you are for a reason, and he put you with this group of believers for a reason. Open up, share the story God has written for your life, and listen with acceptance and honesty as others share. Strive to make your small group a safe place to share and grow in God's love.

READING SCHEDULE
FOR *FEARLESS*

Lesson 1: Chapter 1

Lesson 2: Chapter 2

Lesson 3: Chapter 3

Lesson 4: Chapter 10

Lesson 5: Chapter 13

Lesson 6: Chapter 14

FOR GOD HAS

NOT GIVEN US A

SPIRIT OF FEAR.

2 Timothy 1:7

WHY ARE WE AFRAID?

READ

Read Chapter 1 from *Fearless* before you meet this week.

Fear has touched every one of us in some way—whether it has entangled us or completely enchained us. But how we respond to fear, and whom we turn to for a way out, is what matters more than anything. Will your fear leave you embittered or awestruck? This week's discussion will inspire us to live in awe of Christ, who refused to let fear have any hold on his life—and who wants the same thing for you.

REFLECT

Answer the questions in this section before you meet this week.

Oversized and rude, fear is unwilling to share the heart with happiness. Happiness complies. Do you ever see the two together? Can one be happy and afraid at the same time? Fear is the big bully in the high school hallway: brash, loud, and unproductive. Despite all the noise fear makes and all the room it takes, fear does little good. It's not creative or productive, yet we allow it so much control over our lives. Happiness would be a much better companion.

+ In what ways are fear and happiness able (or unable) to coexist?

Matthew remembered the pouncing tempest and bouncing boat and was careful in his terminology when he wrote his gospel. This storm was a *seismos*—"a trembling eruption of sea and sky." This word is only used two other times—at Jesus' death and at his resurrection. Apparently, the stilled storm shares equal billing in the trilogy of Jesus' great shake-ups. In these moments of *seismos* God reveals something about his character to our fearful souls.

✦ Meditate on these three events and the connection Matthew makes. What is the significance of using the same word at all three instances? What do we learn about God in each story?

The story of the disciples on the boat ends with the not-so-subtle and not-too-popular reminder: getting on board with Christ can mean getting soaked with Christ. Disciples can expect rough seas and stout winds. Christ-followers contract malaria, bury children, and battle addiction, and, as a result, face fears.

+ Why is life filled with trouble for Christians? What makes pain and anguish different for Christians?

Write a brief sentence about how each of these verses has been true (or not true) in your experience.

+ Matthew 9:2: "Take courage, son; your sins are forgiven" (NASB).

+ Luke 12:32: "Do not fear, little flock, for it is your Father's good pleasure to give you the kingdom."

+ Luke 8:50: "Don't be afraid. Just believe, and your daughter will be well" (NCV).

+ Matthew 24:6: "You will hear of wars and rumors of wars, but see to it that you are not alarmed" (NIV).

DISCUSS

Engage in conversation about these questions within your small group.

You may not be down to your final heartbeat, but you may be down to your last paycheck, solution, or thimble of faith. Each sunrise seems to bring fresh reasons for fear. Each of us can find reasons to be afraid, no matter how "good" our life is—no one is immune to fear.

+ What causes your heartbeat to race, your palms to sweat? What makes you afraid?

Fear never wrote a symphony or poem, negotiated a peace treaty, or cured a disease. Fear never pulled a family out of poverty or a country out of bigotry. Fear never saved a marriage or a business. Courage did that. Faith did that. People who refused to consult with or cower to their timidities did that.

+ When, in your experience, has courage overcome fear to accomplish something good?

We hope for an easy ride through life once we meet Christ, smooth sailing on a crystal clear sea. But storms rise up. None of us can escape this inevitable fact—whether we are Christ-followers or not. It's not the absence of storms that sets us apart. It's whom we discover in the storm: an unstirred Christ. He handles our great quakings with a great calming.

+ Describe a time when your life was in chaos, but you could clearly see that Jesus was unstirred by the storm.

As the waves rocked and shook the boat, the disciples screamed and Jesus dreamed. He rested his head not on a fluffy feather pillow but on a leather sandbag. A ballast bag. This was a premeditated slumber. In full knowledge of the coming storm, Jesus decided it was siesta time, so he crawled to the corner, put his head on the pillow, and drifted into dreamland.

+ Have you ever felt that Jesus was sleeping through the storms in your life? How did you respond—in anger, in frustration, in hurt, or with understanding?

+ Does it bring you comfort to know that this reaction is intentional on his part, not accidental or ignorant? If not, how *does* it make you feel?

Fear feels dreadful. It sucks the life out of the soul, curls us into an embryonic state, and drains us dry of contentment. We become abandoned barns, rickety and tilting from the winds, a place where humanity used to eat, thrive, and find warmth. No longer. When fear shapes our lives, safety becomes our god. When safety becomes our god, we worship the risk-free life. Can the safety lover do anything great? Can the risk-averse accomplish noble deeds? For God? For others?

+ Think about the description of a fear-laden person as an "abandoned barn." Give another illustration of how you feel when fear invades your life on a daily, even hourly, basis.

+ To what extent is it okay to pay attention to concerns of safety? Describe the point at which sensible caution becomes worship of a risk-free life.

The disciples on the storm-tossed boat on the Sea of Galilee marveled at Jesus' power. *What kind of man is this?* they thought. And likewise, I wondered at my dad's calm when the Wolf Man lurked behind the couch in my living room when I was six years old. A loving Father, God handles our great storms with great calm.

+ In what ways have your encounters with fear increased your awe of God?

+ Describe a time when Jesus spoke to the storm in your life, and the winds calmed and the waves stilled.

WRAP UP

Over the course of the next week, remind yourself of God's track record in your life. Journal in the space provided about the times he has calmed the storms in your life. When you find yourself struggling against fear, pull this list out and remind yourself that God is capable.

MEMORY VERSE

"Do not fear, little flock, for it is your Father's good pleasure to give you the kingdom."

Luke 12:32

PRAYER REQUESTS

NOTES

NOTES

So don't be
afraid. You are
worth much
more than many
sparrows.

Matthew 10:31 NCV

FEAR OF NOT MATTERING

READ

Read Chapter 2 from *Fearless* before you meet this week.

Each of us wants to matter—whether we strive for international fame or simply desire the love and respect of those we know. And when we find we have been overlooked, forgotten, or abandoned, it hurts deeply. The truth, no matter how we feel, is that we are deeply important to God. But it's not based on anything we do—we matter to God because we are his creation. Doesn't that take the pressure off?

REFLECT

Answer the questions in this section before you meet this week.

You are God's idea. Indeed, his best idea. He calls you his masterpiece. So when you believe you're worth nothing, you'll never matter, your life won't make a difference, you're second-guessing his decision. You're insulting his creation.

+ Read the following verses and write a brief statement under each one about your value in God's eyes.

Psalm 139:14–15

Psalm 139:18

Ephesians 2:10

Matthew 10:29–31

LESSON 2

FEAR OF NOT MATTERING

+ Where do you draw the line between humility and viewing yourself as valueless? How does each attitude impact your relationship with God?

Read the letter on pages 26–27 of *Fearless* about the movie *Hook*. Listen. God is talking to you. Do you hear? He's looking into your face, finding the beauty the years bury, the sparkle that time tries to take. Seeing you and loving the you he sees. "There you are. There you are!" he says.

+ Which relationships, jobs, journeys, or heartbreaks have taken some of the sparkle from your eyes?

+ What would it take to have that beauty restored? (You will discuss this further with the group when you meet.)

DISCUSS

Engage in conversation about these questions within your small group.

+ Read Matthew 10:31 out loud as a group and take a poll: do you feel that God cares deeply about you as an individual?

We all find ways to make ourselves important. My childhood friend Thomas snagged Dean Martin's cigarette butt at a celebrity golf tournament, and having it gave him importance in his fourth-grade community. Ultimately we believe, "Connect to someone special and become someone special, right?"

+ Is the philosophy of being special by association present (or even prevalent) in your life? Explain.

We fear nothingness, insignificance. We fear evaporation. We fear that in the last tabulation we make no contribution to the final sum. We fear coming and going and no one knowing. That's why it bothers us when a friend forgets to call or a colleague takes credit for something we've done. They are affirming our deepest trepidation: no one cares.

+ Describe a time in which you've been hurt by feeling that you do not matter.

+ Have you ever hurt another person by communicating to them that they were valueless?

There is a connection between our desire to matter and our desire for new, stylish clothes: Fashion redeems us from the world of littleness and nothingness, and we are something else. Why? Because we spent half a paycheck on a pair of Italian jeans. But then, horror of horrors, the styles change and we're left wearing yesterday's jeans, feeling like yesterday's news.

+ Fashion is only one example of how we try to make ourselves significant. What are some things you do to make yourself feel important?

God reassures us, in Matthew 10:29–31, of our significance to him. And in Luke's Gospel Jesus goes a tender step further: "Are not five sparrows sold for two pennies? And not one of them is forgotten before God" (12:6 RSV). One penny would buy you two sparrows. Two pennies, however, would buy you five. The merchant throws in a fifth sparrow for free. But God still remembers him.

+ Have you ever felt like a fifth sparrow—indistinct, dispensable, disposable, worthless?

+ As you reflect on these emotions, do you feel motivated to help those fifth sparrows who need reminders of God's deep love for them?

The fear that you are one big zero will become a self-fulfilling prophecy that will ruin your life. It creates the result it dreads, arrives at the destination it tries to avoid, facilitates the scenario it disdains. If you pass your days mumbling that you'll never matter, guess what? You'll be sentencing yourself to a life of gloom without parole.

+ Describe a time when fear of insignificance sabotaged your dreams.

+ Looking back, what would you have done differently in that situation?

FEARLESS

Read aloud the letter on pages 26–27 of *Fearless* (about the movie *Hook*). God is saying the same words to you. Finding the beauty the years bury, the sparkle that time tries to take. Seeing you and loving the you he sees. "There you are. There you are!"

+ What has buried your beauty? What will it take for your sparkle to shine again?

WRAP UP

God is enough, isn't he? Let others play the silly games. Not us. We've found something better. This week, quit clamoring for fulfillment, and instead abandon your self-fulfilling fears at the feet of the One who truly matters. Journal about your experience in the space provided below.

FEARLESS

MEMORY VERSE

"For we are God's masterpiece. He has created us anew in Christ Jesus, so we can do the good things he planned for us long ago."

Ephesians 2:10 NLT

PRAYER REQUESTS

NOTES

NOTES

TAKE COURAGE,

SON; YOUR SINS

ARE FORGIVEN.

Matthew 9:2 NASB

FEAR OF DISAPPOINTING GOD

READ

Read Chapter 3 from *Fearless* before you meet this week.

You may think you have no access to God—that you have disappointed him beyond repair. But it's not true! If you fear you have blown it, take heart in these words: "Yes, you failed. We've all failed. But you aren't a failure. God came for people like us." This week you will have a chance to hand your embarrassments, failures, and regrets to God so you can start again with a clean slate, trusting him to love you despite your past.

REFLECT

Answer the questions in this section before you meet this week.

Noble Doss was a successful college and professional football player. In his college career he dropped a pass that cost his team a trip to the Rose Bowl, and although he has accomplished great things in his athletic career since that moment, it's still something he thinks about with deep sadness and embarrassment every day.

+ Do you have a mistake or embarrassment that you think of daily?

LESSON 3

Embracing the perfect forgiveness that is ours through Christ can be a daily struggle. When Jesus healed the paralytic man in Matthew 9, he didn't simply heal the man's legs. He also bolstered the man's hope when he announced that his sins were forgiven.

+ Do you hope for your sins to be forgiven—or are you looking for something more temporary (legs that won't walk, for example) to be healed?

+ If you answered, "No, I don't worry about the forgiveness of my sins," look a little deeper. Is it possible that sin is at the root of your other problems?

In the garden of Eden, the serpent tempted Eve; he said that God was unable to deliver what she needed. Eve quit trusting God and took matters—and the fruit—into her own hands.

✦ How did fear inform Eve's actions?

✦ Is there an area of your life where you're holding on too tightly, where you fear God can't provide so you'll have to do it yourself?

DISCUSS

Engage in conversation about these questions within your small group.

Noble Doss was happily married for six decades. He was a father and grandfather. He served in the navy during World War II and appeared on the cover of *Life* magazine with his University of Texas football team. But the memory of one dropped past faded too slowly, a daily disappointment that he never could shake. Fifty years later, his shame still brought him to tears.

✦ Do you live with a regret that you remember often?

◆ What have you done to overcome a pattern of dwelling on past failures?

Many of us fear we have "outsinned" God's patience. "God's well of grace must have a bottom to it," we reason. "A person can request forgiveness only so many times," our common sense contends. "Cash in too many mercy checks, and sooner or later one is going to bounce." The devil loves this line of logic. He wants us to doubt that God really has unconditional love for us, a love that will survive any offense, no matter how often we make it.

✦ You may know in your head that God says he'll always forgive, but does your heart believe it? How does your spirit respond to this?

✦ What do you believe is the devil's role in our fear of disappointing God?

+ How can you think rightly about God's love for you?

To sin is to disregard God, ignore his teachings, deny his blessings. Sin is "God-less" living, centering life on the center letter of the word sIn. The sinner's life is me-focused, not God-focused. And because the sinner's life is focused inward, fear is rampant. A sinful life is absent the bedrock of God's grace, something we will only know when we look toward God.

+ What is your definition of sin?

✦ Is it possible that we can only find real bravery when the problem of sin is solved?

Fear, when mismanaged, leads to sin. Sin leads to hiding. When we know we are wrong, we do not see the One who can do no wrong. So instead we hide—not in bushes like Adam and Eve, but in eighty-hour workweeks, temper tantrums, and religious busyness. We avoid contact with God.

✦ Why is hiding our first response?

✦ What emotion or need does hiding satisfy? What would contact with God truly satisfy?

Jesus loves us too much to leave us in doubt about his grace. His "perfect love expels all fear" (1 John 4:18 NLT). If God loved with an imperfect love, we would have high cause to worry. Imperfect love keeps a list of sins and consults it often. God keeps no list of our wrongs. His love casts out fear because he casts out our sin!

✦ Explore the role faith plays in accepting God's perfect love.

When you feel unforgiven, evict the feelings. Emotions don't get a vote. To welcome them to dinner and invite them to stay the night is to kick God out to the curb. To welcome fear with open arms is to reject Christ's promise of security, love, and life. So, when feelings of doubt and dread creep in, send them packing.

✦ How can you send doubt packing?

WRAP UP

The great news of the gospel is that God's grace is real. Take some time this week to write down the moments in your life when God's grace has given you a clear view of him. Keep this list as a reminder when storm clouds start to gather overhead again.

LESSON 3

FEAR OF DISAPPOINTING GOD

MEMORY VERSE

"He who believes in Him is not condemned."

John 3:18

PRAYER REQUESTS

NOTES

DON'T LET YOUR HEARTS BE
TROUBLED. TRUST IN GOD,
AND TRUST ALSO IN ME. . . .
I WILL COME AND GET YOU,
SO THAT YOU WILL ALWAYS
BE WITH ME WHERE I AM.

John 14:1, 3 NLT

FEAR OF LIFE'S FINAL MOMENTS

READ

Read Chapter 10 from *Fearless* before you meet this week.

We desire to face death unafraid. Impossible? Not when you can view death as a new adventure in existence. Because of Christ, we can face our next life with peace. This week we'll look at the reasons we fear dying and see that as we grow closer to Christ we will not fear death but may even look forward to it with anticipation.

REFLECT

Answer the questions in this section before you meet this week.

We all desire to face death unafraid. To die without fright or a fight . . . perhaps even with a smile. Impossible? Some have said so. But many live as if death is the worst moment in life.

Just look at the revenue the anti-aging industry boasts! We are scared to death of death.

+ What do you fear about death?

This is the promise of Christ: "Don't let your hearts be troubled. Trust in God, and trust also in me. There is more than enough room in my Father's home. If this were not so, would I have told you that I am going to prepare a place for you? When everything is ready, I will come and get you, so that you will always be with me where I am" (John 14:1–3 NLT).

✦ What does this promise mean to you? How does it ease your fears?

✦ Get in the mind-set of a first-century Christian. Think of the challenges they faced and the unknowns they had about heaven, considering the newness of the gospel message. How might this message have affected them differently than it affects us?

Read the following verses and write a few sentences about what you think the afterlife will be like.

John 14:1–3

1 Corinthians 15:23

Revelation 21:15—22:6

DISCUSS

Engage in conversation about these questions within your small group.

✦ Describe a scene from a movie or a book when a character dies peacefully—without fright or a fight. In what ways did that image move you?

Great philosophers throughout history have lamented the passage into death, calling it "the end of everything" and "the great Perhaps." But suppose death is different than they thought, less a curse and more a passageway, not a crisis to be avoided but a corner to be turned? If we change the way we think about death, we will change the way we feel about death.

+ If you are able to remove your association of fear with death, how will your life be changed? Will you live differently?

Ancient Greek philosophy had a despairing view of death: images of the River Styx and the boatman Charon. Upon death, a soul was released into a sunless afterlife of bodiless spirits, shades, and shadows. This was the landscape into which Jesus entered. But he changed our understanding of death forever. He walked into this swamp of uncertainty and built a sturdy bridge. He promised not just an afterlife but a better life.

✦ How did Jesus' promises change human understanding of death? Why was he able to do this?

Jesus frequently used wedding imagery to describe the afterlife, but for most of us the mental pictures of weddings and funerals couldn't be more opposite. Weddings are joyous times of union and new starts—and the thoughts of babies and new life aren't far on the horizon. But funerals seem to be the end of a long journey, or the tragic cutting short of opportunity and love. But Jesus saw it differently.

✦ Why would Jesus use wedding imagery to describe death and the afterlife?

✦ In what ways are you sure of your bridegroom Christ as you think of your next existence with him?

Many of us think of heaven in terms of clouds, winged cherubs, harps, and golden streets. We wonder if we'll have real bodies or if we'll be spirits floating around in the sky. Jesus experienced a physical and factual resurrection. And because he did, we will too! "Christ was raised as the first of the harvest; then all who belong to Christ will be raised when he comes back" (1 Corinthians 15:23 NLT).

✦ Describe your image of heaven. Is it biblical?

Death is not to be feared. Your last moment is not your worst. Charon won't ferry you into oblivion. How do we know? What is our proof? Five hundred witnesses to Jesus' resurrection leave a still-resounding testimony: it's safe to die.

✦ How does Jesus' resurrection make it safe for you to die?

✦ Do you find comfort in the proof of Jesus' resurrection?

Our uncertainty about death—what the afterlife will really be like—generates a lot of our fear about it. We dread the unknown rather than look at it as an opportunity for exploration. Charles Lindbergh wrote these words to be read aloud at his burial service: "Death is a new adventure in existence." No need to dread it or ignore it. Because of Christ, we can face it.

+ We talked last week about our tendency to worship safety. How does letting go of that desire for control influence your fears (or lack thereof) about death?

Comfort with the thought of death is born out of an intimate relationship with God. On the night before my heart surgery, God and I had the most honest of talks (see page 122 of *Fearless*). We began with a good review of my first half century. The details would bore you, but they entertained us. Ultimately, I went to sleep at peace, knowing that it if was my last night on earth, I'd be safe in the arms of my Father the next day.

+ How does enjoying your relationship with God reduce your fear of death and the life to come?

FEARLESS

WRAP UP

Are you at a point where you're comfortable saying, "This could be my final night in this version of life, and if that's the case, I'm okay"? If not, spend time getting to know God's goodness in a personal way. As you get closer to him, you may even find yourself longing for the day you will meet him face-to-face. Journal about your experience in the space provided below.

MEMORY VERSE

"Don't let your hearts be troubled. Trust in God, and trust also in me. There is more than enough room in my Father's home. If this were not so, would I have told you that I am going to prepare a place for you? When everything is ready, I will come and get you, so that you will always be with me where I am."

John 14:1–3 NLT

Prayer Requests

NOTES

YOU WILL HEAR

OF WARS AND

RUMORS OF WARS,

BUT SEE TO IT

THAT YOU ARE

NOT ALARMED.

Matthew 24:6 NIV

FEAR OF GLOBAL CALAMITY

READ

Read Chapter 13 from *Fearless* before you meet this week.

This week we'll explore one of the most prevalent fears around—the fear of global calamity. We hear about it on the news and online. Our friends and neighbors warn us of the latest disaster rumors. Life is a dangerous endeavor. We pass our days in the shadows of ominous realities. But God has diagnosed the pain of the world and written the book on its treatment. We can trust him.

REFLECT

Answer the questions in this section before you meet this week.

The Bible is full of warnings of the dangerous environment we live in. There's no point in pretending everything is just fine, but Jesus also tells us to not be "alarmed," with a modern-translation reading something like, "Don't freak out."

+ What is the difference between being aware of your situation with a rational concern, and being alarmed or freaking out? Where is the fine line between being a realist and being a cynic?

+ How are Christians to handle the onslaught of bad news that streams through our television sets and computer screens every day?

FEAR OF GLOBAL CALAMITY

We're told that we will hear of "wars and rumors of wars" as long as life continues on this planet. But many Christians feel compelled to pray for peace around the globe, specifically in the Middle East.

✦ Do you think prayers for global peace are in vain? Are they sinful? Are they good?

✦ If there will always be wars, what should believers hope and pray for?

During World War II, bombs fell on Poland. But one lone building partly survived the bombs—a wall stood with these words clearly legible from a short distance: "Heaven and earth will pass away, but my words will never pass away."

+ Why must this world pass away?

+ How does the temporary nature of earthly life affect our daily routine? How should our priorities change to be more focused on eternity?

DISCUSS

Engage in conversation about these questions within your small group.

Pharmaceutical companies have invaded our nightly entertainment with their promises of renewed vitality, but they also warn against potential tragedy. There is something about that merger of happy faces with voice-over advisories of paralysis that just doesn't work.

+ Are there paradoxes you see in life, or in the media, that bother you?

Sitting on the Mount of Olives, Jesus issued a "buckle your seat belt, no kidding, life can be fatal to your health" warning. He wanted his followers to know what they were facing, because life with Christ is not necessarily an easy journey. Christ promised he would be there for us on the way, though, and his burden is light because we get to walk step-by-step with him. But he began his lecture with the unexpected words, "Watch out that no one deceives you."

+ When you think of global disaster, do you fear being deceived?

✦ Why do you think Jesus mentioned deception first in his
description of the end of the world?

Jesus told about false teachers that will emerge in the final
days. Don't be wooed by their slick appearances, silver-tongued
oratory, or performances. They'll command multitudes and
miracles. Large audiences and spectacular deeds. Throngs of
people. Displays of power. When you see them, be careful.
High volume doesn't equate with sound faith. Don't be
impressed by numbers or tricks. Satan can counterfeit both.

✦ Have you witnessed false teachers in your spiritual
experience?

America, proud as she is of religious freedom, suffers from increasing anger toward Christians. Professors publicly mock Bible-believing students. Talk-show hosts denigrate people of faith. We can expect persecution to increase. When it does, fragile convictions will collapse.

+ Are you on the front lines in the defense of Christianity, or has your love for God grown cold? What's the evidence?

Real courage embraces the twin realities of current difficulty and ultimate triumph. Christians should live somewhere between Pollyanna and Chicken Little, between blind denial and blatant panic. This world needs levelheaded, clear-thinking, and still-believing followers of Christ who will bring others to focus on God and his grace in a time of tragedy.

+ How does false or empty optimism hurt you more than a realistic evaluation of your situation?

+ "The church" in America has a reputation for expecting Christians to be always positive, but Jesus was brutally honest in his description of terrible things to come. How did we lose that realistic perspective, and why?

FEARLESS

The *Titanic* sank because contractors settled for cheap rivets and planned poorly. Rivets are the glue that hold the steel plates together. Facing a shortage of quality bolts, the builders used substandard ones that popped their heads upon impact with the iceberg.[1] Because of this shortsighted construction, hundreds of people lost their lives in a matter of minutes in the icy waters of the Atlantic Ocean.

+ How sturdy are the bolts of your belief? Take a look at what's happening around the globe. Do you think you could handle the type of persecution that Christians face around the world?

1 William J. Broad, "Scientists' New Findings Link *Titanic*'s Fast Sinking to Rivets," *San Antonio Express-News*, April 15, 2008.

LESSON 5

All things, big and small, flow out of the purpose of God and serve his good will. When the world appears to be out of control, it isn't. We can trust that God is holy, good, loving, and in control. Our vision is limited: what looks like terror might actually be triumph. What looks like heartbreak might actually be healing. We must trust that God is who he says he is.

✦ How can you remind yourself that God is in control?

WRAP UP

Yes, sometimes life stinks. But it won't forever. As one of my friends likes to say, "Everything will work out in the end. If it's not working out, it's not the end." Write a prayer about the things that are not working out in your life today. Take time each day this week to pray the prayer you wrote, and trust God to take care of the concerns you bring to him.

LESSON 5

FEAR OF GLOBAL CALAMITY

MEMORY VERSE

"Be still in the presence of the LORD, and wait patiently
for him to act. Don't worry about evil people who
prosper or fret about their wicked schemes."

Psalm 37:7 NLT

Prayer Requests

NOTES

THEY FELL ON THEIR FACES
AND WERE GREATLY AFRAID.
BUT JESUS CAME AND TOUCHED
THEM AND SAID, "ARISE, AND
DO NOT BE AFRAID."

Matthew 17:6–7

LESSON 6

FEAR OF GOD
GETTING OUT
OF MY BOX

READ

Read Chapter 14 from *Fearless* before you meet this week.

We need to view God in his unearthly glory and get him out of our do-me-a-favor and make-me-a-buck boxes. We need to see God's radiance, because with a Messiah like him, who can fear? This week we'll take a look at the Transfiguration to see how the disciples' images of Jesus were blown to bits when his glory was revealed on a hillside in the holy land.

REFLECT

Answer the questions in this section before you meet this week.

This chapter discusses the events surrounding Jesus' transfiguration, when his closest earthly friends joined him on a Galilean hillside and saw a radically different version of him than they ever expected. He changed from a meek carpenter to a Being of divine light. It was a life-changing moment for these three men.

+ Imagine yourself at the scene. How do you think you would have responded to the events of that day?

Think back over each of the topics you've studied in this book—fear of not mattering, of disappointing God, of life's final moments, of global calamity, and of God getting out of your box.

+ Which fear was the strongest in your life when you started this study?

+ Which has changed the most as a result of going through this workbook?

◆ Do you feel equipped to help others with their fears as a result of having completed this study?

DISCUSS

Engage in conversation about these questions within your small group.

A taxi driver in Brazil rubs the plastic miniature Jesus on his dashboard when he needs a parking space, calling on his do-me-a-favor Jesus. The late-night cable TV preacher asks for your money, trusting in the make-me-a-buck Jesus. Our sin tempts us to conjure different genie Jesuses when we need a favor or a good-luck charm, but it is devastating to our faith to reinforce a false view of God.

+ In what ways have you reduced Jesus down to a handful of doctrines, attempting to fit him into the boxes of your life?

Box-sized gods. You'll find them in the tight grip of people who prefer a god they can manage, control, and predict. This topsy-turvy life requires a tame deity, doesn't it? In a world out of control, we need a god we can control, a comforting presence akin to a lap dog or the kitchen cat. We call and he comes. We pet and he purrs. *If we can just keep God in his place . . .*

+ Many of us don't want excessive amounts of responsibility—having the job of U.S. president, for example. Nevertheless, we try to control God. Why?

All through the gospels we see the divinely human Jesus—a meek man with compassion and conviction who hailed from a village on the outskirts of town. But at the Transfiguration, Christ was his truest self, wearing his pre-Bethlehem and post-resurrection wardrobe. Not "a pale Galilean, but a towering and furious figure who will not be managed."[2]

+ Do you tend to think of Jesus more as a "pale Galilean" or the "furious figure"?

+ How does being a "furious figure who will not be managed" fit with Jesus' crucifixion?

---

2 Thomas Howard, *Christ the Tiger* (Philadelphia: J. B. Lippincott, 1967), 10.

As Peter, James, and John witnessed Jesus' divine transformation, we can't help but wonder about their frame of mind. Their friend and daily companion was radically transformed into something larger than life, something divine, something glorious. Don't we half-expect them to repeat their Sea of Galilee question: "What kind of man is this?"

+ Do you think we have any chance of grasping Jesus' glory without witnessing it firsthand?

+ What has to happen before God will get out of the box you've created for him?

Most of our fears are poisonous. They steal sleep and pillage peace. But fear of the Lord is different. As awe of Jesus expands, fears of life diminish. A big God translates into a big courage. A small view of God generates no courage.

+ How long has it been since a fresh understanding of Christ has buckled your knees and emptied your lungs with awe?

+ When times get tough, how can you foster a correct view of God?

We need to know the transfigured Christ. The One who spits holy fires. Who convenes and commands historical figures. Who occupies the loftiest perch and wears only the true crown of the universe. God's beloved Son.

+ How do we get to know the transfigured Christ?

+ What have you learned over the last six weeks about the connection between our relationship with God, our understanding of him, and our fears?

WRAP UP

Take an inventory of your faith expectations, journaling in the space provided below. Discard your boxes and old images of Christ like used tissues. Watch your arrogant certainty become meek curiosity. You may just find yourself falling on your face in awe like the disciples did.

LESSON 6

FEAR OF GOD GETTING OUT OF MY BOX

MEMORY VERSE

"Arise, and do not be afraid."

Matthew 17:7

Prayer Requests

NOTES

Experience the Central Message of the Christian Faith!

This dynamic study for small groups brings together the compelling 3:16 Bible Study Guide, which explores some of the most important take-aways and truths from the 3:16 book, along with the Stories of Hope DVD, featuring 12 sessions, filled with Max Lucado's insight and inspiration. The Kit also contains evangelism tools, leader's guide, and promotional materials to engage your small group like never before! Join Max Lucado as he unpacks this timeless message- phrase by phrase.

The 3:16 New Testament with Psalms & Proverbs is a beautifully inspiring gift for a friend, loved one, or even yourself. Invite others to encounter the 3:16 God who longs to offer true life through His Son, Jesus Christ.

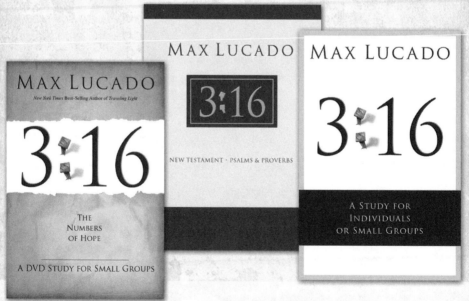

Available wherever books and Bibles are sold
To learn more, visit www.nelsonbibles.com

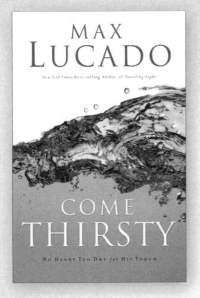

You don't have to live with a dehydrated heart. God invites you to treat your thirsty soul as you would treat your physical thirst. Just visit the WELL and drink deeply:

Receive Christ's **Work** on the cross,
The **Energy** of his Spirit,
His **Lordship** over your life,
And his unending, unfailing **Love**.

Come thirsty, and drink the water of **life**.

In the *Come Thirsty DVD Study*,
Max Lucado takes you and your
small group on a six-week journey
to explore the WELL of God's love.
Leader's Guide included.

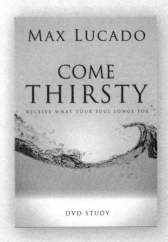

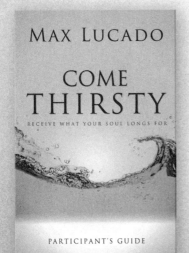

This conversational discussion guide is perfect for small group use in combination with the *Come Thirsty DVD Study*, and includes:

+ Exploration of the WELL of God's love: Work, Energy, Lordship, and Love

+ Six weeks of community-building questions and discussion starters

+ A reading plan for Max Lucado's bestseller *Come Thirsty*

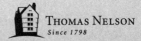

THOMAS NELSON
Since 1798

NOW THAT YOU ARE FEARLESS, YOU ARE READY TO FACE YOUR GIANTS

The same God who helped David slay Goliath will help you.

Focus on Giants—You Stumble
Focus on God—Your Giants Tumble

• AVAILABLE NOW •

WWW.MAXLUCADO.COM

THE CAMPAIGN TO MAKE
POVERTY HISTORY
WWW.ONE.ORG

There is a plague of biblical proportions taking place in Africa right now, but we can beat this crisis, if we each do our part. Step ONE is signing the ONE petition, to join the ONE Campaign.

The ONE Campaign is a new effort to rally Americans—ONE by ONE—to fight global AIDS and extreme poverty. We are engaging Americans everywhere we gather—in churches and synagogues, on the internet and college campuses, at community meetings and concerts. To learn more about The ONE Campaign, go to www.one.org and sign the online petition.

> "Use your uniqueness to take great risks for God! If you're great with kids, volunteer at the orphanage. If you have a head for business, start a soup kitchen. If God bent you toward medicine, dedicate a day or a decade to AIDS patients. The only mistake is not to risk making one."
>
> —Max Lucado, *Cure for the Common Life*

ONE Voice can make a difference.
Let God work through you; join the ONE Campaign now!

This campaign is brought to you by

You could be the answer to a child's prayer. When you sponsor a child you will be providing things like food, shelter, clothing, clean water, education, and hope for a brighter future.

Become a Sponsor, Help Change a
Life

Visit www.maxlucado.com/worldvision
for more information on how to sponsor
a child and additional ways to give.

World Vision®
Building a better world for children